Killing My Father.

Then Finding Him

Life Observations by John Harrell

This book is dedicated to my good friend, Mark Lehman. Without Mark's encouragement, nudging and pestering, I would not have written anything.

Preface

Searching for meaning and purpose in life is nothing new. We come to a place where we question why we are here. We want our lives to matter, to count for something and fill the void we feel. The 17th century French philosopher Pascal described the void as a "God-shaped vacuum." By definition, a vacuum is an emptiness. What a perfect way to describe the feeling we get when we 'awaken' and begin the quest to find our purpose.

For some of us, before we could truly live we had to get rid of the voices from the past. In the depths of our souls we refuse to give up, no longer seduced to believe the lies we were told in our youth by harmful parents. The two people who are supposed to be the most important influences in our lives, at least during our early years, have sabotaged our futures. In my case, my mother and father told me I "wasn't worth a damn; I would never amount to anything." Imagine the conflict of believing their lies while trying not to, then finding the inner strength to overcome my painful upbringing and create a meaningful, purpose-filled life. It has been a battle.

I often say, when I'm struggling I'm growing. I'm struggling all the time! Giving up and giving in means accepting your circumstances and coasting through life; just existing. We were built for purpose and we were built for speed. All of us. So many people I meet have dynamic dreams for their futures and talk passionately about fulfilling their life's purpose. What stops them? What I am finding is we share similar backgrounds, but they still believe the lies.

Everyone has a faith life. Even atheists believe in something-themselves. My spiritual life was dormant for decades and consisted of calling on God when I was in trouble and needed immediate help. Afterward God could take His usual place on the backburner, go help someone else, and I could take it from there. That changed in May 2013 when I had what I call my second encounter with Jesus Christ. Yep, that guy. My life has taken a new trajectory since then, albeit slowly at times, where I find meaning for my existence. I didn't start dressing weird, stand on a street corner with a sign warning people to repent, nor did I walk around shouting "Praise the Lord." No, I am the same man but with hope for a better, purpose-filled future.

The purpose of this book is not to convert you, challenge your beliefs or be judgmental. You don't have to be a Christian to be a good person. The purpose of this writing is to encourage you while giving you the tools to begin the journey to overcome a painful past, forgive those who harmed you and start living. Believing in God is not required to accomplish this. My faith is part of my story. You must write your own. Killing my father is a metaphor which describes killing the voices that spoke lies to me for years. You will learn how I came to forgive my parents and accept them for who they were, failings and all. For the readers who had ideal parents, my hope is you will find greater joy when you remember your youth. You weren't raised the way I was, and for that my other hope is you will view your life with gratitude.

When the disciples asked Jesus to “teach us to pray” (Luke 11:1 NIV), the first word out of Jesus’ mouth was “Father.” Sometimes I wish Jesus had used a different word. Calling God, who is perfect, father is difficult to reconcile for those of us with less-than-perfect fathers. We can’t help but project our earthly fathers onto God the Father. For many of us that’s really uncomfortable. Finding my father is learning the character of God, who He is, dispelling the lies I assumed about Him and seeing Him differently than my earthly father.

For the readers who relate to an ugly childhood, I encourage you to take the steps to kill the voices. Change is hard. Keep your eyes focused on a new, more fulfilling and meaningful life. It’s a process, never an arrival point. Just begin…

Table of Contents

Faith

Is God real? Does He exist? Fair questions, and I believe most of us have wrestled with belief in a God of any type at some point in our lives. We are taught God is love, yet how can a loving God allow so much pain and suffering in the world? Any given day we see starving people, death, incurable diseases, broken families, children sold into sex slavery and more. Where is a God in this mess?

Faith is a difficult jumping off point. Faith means something different to almost everyone. For some, their only faith is in themselves. Yet we demonstrate faith every day when we fill up our gas tanks, hoping the gas we put in our cars is pure and not tainted with another substance. Flying from one destination to another we have faith the pilot knows how to fly. Even when we drive we have faith the other drivers will obey the law and stop when they are supposed to. Just because we are not consciously aware we are practicing faith in these situations doesn't make it less real.

Discussing faith with others can be messy, because how we interpret faith's meaning is subjective. One area about faith we all agree on is when we see heinous acts caused by perversion of faith. For example, ISIS has tortured and killed hundreds of thousands of Christians, Muslims, Mandaeans and Yazidis. We want no part of whatever ISIS believes in! Gross perversion of faith is nothing new. In Old Testament days, the Prophets of Ba'al believed in sacrificing *children,* and they did.

We ask, where is God when the innocence of a child is taken from them? Their once beautiful, hope-filled lives with dreams of a bright future are shattered when they are sold into sex slavery. Or the girl who is in the wrong place at the wrong time and is raped? Hope is replaced with hopelessness, and we are supposed to rely on a God who allowed this to happen to be our beacon of hope and promise? Was He around when the Prophets of Ba'al were sacrificing children? Yes, He was there, weeping with everyone who suffered and with those who suffer today. So, why does He allow it when He has the power to stop it? Legitimate question, and I will return to it.

A few years ago, my pastor Dr. Dave Haney gave a message describing the four ways we experience God's presence. I will do my best to share some of it with you here.

The first way we experience God's presence is through our instincts. Yes, our instincts. Our instincts aren't infallible, and we don't want to rely solely on them, but that doesn't make them less relevant. Have you ever felt something strongly that told you not to do something? It didn't feel right? That is your instincts talking to you. Have you done it, whatever it is, only to have it turn out badly? In hindsight, should've listened. The same can be said when you feel strongly about something that feels right. Don't count your instincts out.

Another way to experience our Creator is through the Bible. I used to think the Bible was boring, so I avoided it. Then I discovered how interesting some of the characters and stories were. After I learned there were Bibles in plain English I started reading it. I try to read something every day, even if its just a little bit. Most days I get nothing from reading Scripture, so I put it away, only to return the next day. No need to force anything. Then one day I'm reading something and the words practically jump off the page at me. It's like this piece was written *just for me.* What is more remarkable are the times I'm reading something I've read before, but this time it resonates with me. This is when God shows up. I never know when He will, so that is why I keep coming back. I call this putting myself in a position to succeed. Every single time it happens my mind is blown.

Other people are a third way we experience God...if we are *listening.* Example: I was discussing the idea for this book with two of my friends, laying out my vision, who it might reach, how the message could impact others, when one of my friends suggested another way to look at what I planned to write. Immediately, my vision crystallized, and I knew which way to go. Had I not listened to a friend I trust, this idea would be floundering in chaos! That was God speaking to me through a friend.

Several years ago, I was having a conversation with a client who is a brilliant scientist. At one point, we started talking about faith. My client said, "You know, as a scientist, I'm really sort of an atheist. I believe in what I can demonstrate scientifically and I'm not sure that includes a deity." I replied, "Okay, I get that. But consider this. Have you ever experienced love?" "Of course!" he replied. Then I asked him to write out the scientific formula for love. He smiled, but obviously couldn't comply. I said, "That's what faith looks like." Since our conversation, the scientist told me he has been on a mission to find God after *listening* to me. I am convinced God was speaking through me to him because I have no idea where asking him to write down the formula for love came from! I'm not that good when left to my own devices.

The fourth, and for me the best, way to experience the existence of God comes from examining our lives forensically; looking backwards. When I perform this examination of moments from my past, I see God was guiding me. I admit it didn't feel like He was in the same city as me during some of the storms I have gone through. But He was there. This gives me hope for the future. I know difficulties will come, but I will rely on a Higher Power to guide me through. Make no mistake here, faith is a verb; an action word. We must do something and not sit around waiting for everything to be handled for us.

Faith does not come easily for me. It is something I work at, connecting my head to my heart. I am human, perfectly imperfect at best. I'm not alone in having to work at faith. Consider Jesus' disciples. They were along for the ride and witnessed countless miracles. Eyesight was restored to the blind, the sick healed, demons exorcised, and dead people brought back to life, just to name a few. They were *there* but scattered in fear when Jesus was arrested. The disciples are the last people you would think would be filled with doubt and fear. Jesus warned them about this, saying, "Your faith will be shaken (Mark 14:27 NIV)." I believe Jesus' was saying this to us, too. After Jesus' resurrection their faith was restored. Many of the disciples died horrible deaths because of their now *unshakeable faith.*

Faith, according to the Merriam-Webster online dictionary, is defined as "firm belief in something for which there is no proof." Faith sounds a little like love, doesn't it?

Back to the question posed earlier, why does God allow horrible, unthinkable things to happen? I will venture out onto the very thin ice and offer this: God can't cause evil (yes, there are things God cannot do) because of His immutable good character, but He can bring good from it. When a child weeps, God weeps with him. God doesn't want a girl taken from her home and family, only to be sold into sex slavery. He feels everything we feel. Tragedy can be turned into good when we cling to and trust Him. When something horrible has happened, we may not feel like trusting. It's hard, but He is patient. Painful, unimaginable grieving can open us up to coming closer to God when we're *ready.* And we must leave the judging to Him. He will be just.

In a later chapter, you will read about Rachel's Challenge. Rachel's Challenge is a beautiful example of taking tragedy and using it for good. Stay tuned...

Judgment

On June 12, 2016 a gunman entered Pulse Nightclub in Orlando, Florida with the intent to murder. Before his shooting spree ended, Omar Matoon, only 29 years old, had killed 49 people and sent 53 more to the hospital. The brutality of his crime is unimaginable. The floor of the nightclub became a pool of blood. Matoon was shot and killed by the Orlando Police Department after a three-hour standoff, leaving so many people asking why...

In the aftermath of the massacre, at least two pastors issued statements. One said, "The tragedy is that more of them didn't die. I'm kind of upset he didn't finish the job." Another pastor said the Pulse Nightclub patrons were "getting what they deserved." Pulse Nightclub was a gay club. No words.

Considering the cruelty of those two statements, it makes sense why fewer and fewer people are attending church. I would not attend their churches. The people who are supposed to be the first-responders of healing were spewing judgment and vitriol. I cannot imagine what family members, friends and co-workers of the dead and injured must have felt when they heard those statements. Judgment was handed down by two people who are in no position to judge anyone. The patrons who had the misfortune of being at Pulse that evening were *people*, and the God I know doesn't play favorites because you're straight. They did not "get what they deserved."

Judging others is a heart problem. If someone disagrees with you, it's fine. Lashing out in anger, insulting others along with self-righteousness because you believe your values have been challenged is never okay. With the onslaught of opinions on social media, we have witnessed an ugly side of people. Our divide in Washington, D.C. is alive and active between the Republican and Democratic parties. If you see a Congressman on television, you will see 'R 'or 'D' associated with their name. That indicator is there to let you know whether you need to listen to them or not (Sarcasm). Therein lies the problem, we aren't listening to those with whom we may disagree. Does it have to be this way? Can't we learn from each other, make each other better? I believe we can.

In the 1980's, President Reagan and House Speaker Thomas P. "Tip" O'Neill couldn't stand each other. It has been said they hated each other. Yet the two political adversaries found a way to forge a solid working partnership which placed the needs of our country above politics and party. Both men stayed true to their values but found common ground from which they could work. Each man realized they needed each other to save the country from the worst recession since the Great Depression and were big enough to put aside their personal differences.

When Reagan was shot, O'Neill came to Reagan's bedside in the hospital and they prayed together. In 1986, O'Neill's beloved Boston College decided to build a library in honor of Speaker O'Neill. A fundraising dinner was held at the Washington Hilton (where Reagan had been shot) and the keynote speaker was...Ronald Reagan! Think about that-a popular Republican president speaking at a fundraiser for a political foe. Would that, could that happen today?

Gossip is judgment. The root of judgment is an insecurity in ourselves. Gossiping about others is a feeble attempt to make ourselves look better. Maybe it would be better if we used the energy it takes to gossip to work on our character defects, then gossip goes away. You start to lift others up rather than tear them down. When someone is talking to you about someone else, be assured they are talking to someone else about you. Gossip is harmful to others, and to you. The next time you feel compelled to gossip, consider how you feel when others gossip about you. We don't want to be the subjects of gossip, no more than we desire to be judged.

Two people can look at the same thing and come up with two different perspectives. The constant is the same, only the perspective is different. Who is right in this example? They both are, yet they will fight each other over it.

Jesus did not hold others in judgment. He did call out the hypocrites, and He called them out harshly without mincing words. He knew we would struggle with judging others, so He spoke about it often. Remember the girl caught in the act of adultery? The self-serving, self-righteous crowd of men brought her to Jesus and threw her down in front of Him, further shaming her. One of the people in the crowd decided to cite the law for Jesus and told Him under the law the woman was to be stoned to death. What do you say, Jesus?

Get this image planted firmly in your mind. Here is a young woman, humiliated, probably wearing no more than a bedsheet in full display in front of a crowd who is demanding her immediate death by stoning. I imagine she is crying, trying to get her thoughts together as she replays the day's events through her mind, scared to death about what is to come. As the crowd awaited Jesus' reply, He calmly wrote in the sand. We don't know what He wrote, nor do we know for how long a period He wrote. When He finished, He stood up and said, "The one without sin should cast the first stone." This was the ultimate mic drop. One by one, the crowd dissipated, leaving Jesus with the young woman. He asked, "Who has condemned you?" "No one, sir," was her reply. Then Jesus told her He wouldn't condemn her, either. Jesus didn't judge her, and He certainly could have. He restored and redeemed her in a beautiful act of kindness known as grace.

All of us have fallen short of perfection. None of us has all the facts. Maybe we should not be too hard on others, show a little grace to them instead of being so quick to jump on our judgmental, self-righteous soapbox. Isn't that how we would like to be treated?

Leave the judging to God. He's the only one qualified anyway.

Connection

In November 1956, Nikita Khrushchev, leader of the (then) Soviet Union, said of the United States, "We will take you over without ever firing a shot; we will bury you." Was Khrushchev onto something we couldn't foresee? Our divisiveness is destroying us from within, and the only weapons used are **W**ords of **M**ass **D**estruction. It doesn't have to end this way.

Entropy is the state of going from order to disorder. There are some things we cannot stop, such as aging, but we can stop polluting our minds with wrongful thoughts about people. I believe we can reverse the path we are on and prevent the destruction of a one-time kind, decent society. We can lead with kindness and compassion. It begins with *willingness*. We must be open and willing to connect with each other, even those with whom we disagree.

We have a heart problem in our world. We see it manifested through unthinkable acts of violence and hateful prejudice. People everywhere say they want "unity" and "diversity." Unity and diversity are nice, novel ideas, but they don't resolve the underlying problem. Unity makes one cautious to be themselves and stand apart from the unified group, while diversity divides us further. We should strive for connectedness. Connecting with others means we see through the other person; we peer inside their heart to see them for who they are, not the image we hold of them. We let down our own guards so they can see us, too. We allow the images we hold of each other to be stripped away when we connect. Connection resolves societal divisions political correctness feebly tries to address. Issues like racism, bigotry, hatred, persecuting others for being different, even bullying dissolves when we connect.

Do you recall how united we were after 9/11? There was an overwhelming sense of patriotism in the United States. We had been attacked, and we were going after the bastards who did this to us. It seemed our country, our people had one single goal.

Not so fast, though. We were together as one people unless you were a Muslim. Anti-Muslim hate crimes exploded. It was guilt by association. The 3.3 million Muslims who are American citizens were excluded from the patriotic spirit of the day. Muslims who lived and worked here, paying taxes, sending their children to school and obeying the law were subjected to extreme hate and prejudice. All because of 19 people who had perverted their faith. It was a black mark on our country that should have never happened.

Fast forward to the fall of 2015. After multiple radicals had harmed innocent people, anti-Muslim hate crimes reached levels not seen since the post-9/11 era. There was the idea of collecting a database of American Muslims, a National Muslim Registry if you will, being floated out there. This is outrageous! And it is unthinkable something like this could be considered in the United States!

According to PolitiFact (November 24, 2015), then-candidate Trump, when asked about implementing a National Muslim Registry, didn't give an affirmative answer to the question, but he didn't deny it either. By not quashing the idea in that moment, he was giving implicit permission to the crazies to continue their anti-Muslim prejudice, and they did. He missed what could have been a great leadership moment.

Candidate Clinton wasn't any better when broached about the idea. "We need American Muslims to be our eyes and ears on our front lines" was her statement. Another leadership moment failure.

Nobody suggested creating a Christian Registry. Christians commit crimes, too. Christians blow up abortion clinics, and there were many Christians who turned their heads away when witnessing the unbelievable, heinous crimes Hitler committed. Albert Einstein once said, "The world is a dangerous place to live, not because of the people who are evil, but because of the people who don't do anything about it."

I consider myself fortunate to have a wide variety of friends, covering the spectrum of race, religion and political leanings. I even have a friend who is a pagan worshipper (Seriously, although to my knowledge she hasn't performed a sacrificial offering. Yet!). We recognize, embrace and appreciate our different backgrounds and opinions, engage in spirited conversations yet our friendship withstands the test of conflict. Our values have not been threatened, nor have we compromised them for sake of peaceful resolution. We recognize we get the ability to see the world through different eyes and our thoughts are shaped in an open-minded way. In a word...we connect!

Can we stop the entropy of humanity, decency and decorum? Yes, I believe we can. We must! Viewing the world through the prism of being an eternally optimistic man, I admit my view may be skewed. But I gain hope from the intense conversations I have with friends.

All of us have dynamic personalities, yet we find multiple ways to connect and bridge our differences without sacrificing the relationship. We don't hold each other in judgment which creates healthy dialogue. We learn from each other and recognize our differences can make us better.

Test your convictions. Challenge yourself to open your mind and your heart and see things from other perspectives. Reach out to someone different from you. Look into their heart and let them see you for who you are. Who knows? You might make a connection!

Fear

I grew up in a home filled with fear. We were afraid of my father, afraid of the future and afraid to express ourselves. When I reflect on this, oftentimes I say, half joking yet half serious, it is nothing short of a miracle I did not turn out to be a sociopath. When you study the life of sociopaths, there are similarities in our stories.

My father was unpredictable, volatile, angry and *cruel*. He could change in an instant, going from reading his Bible one moment to tearing his belt off to punish me for spilling something the next. No love was expressed by family members in my home. We didn't know how to show love because it was not shown to us. The idea of a loving family was one I held onto dearly, but as a small child I lacked the tools to manifest it. I became a "performer" to feel a modicum of acceptance and, sometimes, praise.

My mother was horrible at keeping our home clean. In my very young five-year-old mind, I believed this was one reason my dad was angry. He hated coming home to a filthy house, and who could blame him? My mother didn't work outside the home, so it was reasonable to expect a clean house. At five, I took on the job of keeping the house clean. I vacuumed, dusted, did laundry, took out the trash and any other job I noticed needed attention. I loved the short-lived praise I received but imagine my confusion when my dad remained the same guy. So, I worked *harder* at keeping the house straight and clean. No change in his behavior, but our house was clean.

When I was six, I added cooking to the mix. In my young, unaware mind I thought by cooking good meals my dad would be happy. My mom was not very good in the kitchen, so that's how I connected the two. My motive for cooking and cleaning was simple. I wanted a happy family, like the families I saw on television. They didn't yell at each other. When the TV families shared meals together, they talked, nicely, to each other. Watching scripted families celebrating holidays was the worst. Everything just worked perfectly in the created world I observed. I wanted this so badly as a young boy. I took the job on myself to try to create it yet faced huge disappointment when nothing changed. I was frustrated beyond belief, more confused than ever. An odd thing about my dad were the times he would see a close, happy family on television and he would say, "That's how he wants us to be." I would feel hopeful in these moments, only to be let down when his *actions* didn't change. This was the beginning of my feelings of hopelessness. I had a long road ahead of me to reach adulthood. When you are six, one year seems like a lifetime and I had twelve to go until I could leave and create a different life.

I spent much time alone as a child. In isolation I could find some peace. This has carried over into adulthood. I have no problem being alone when I must be. At the same time, I love being with people, whether it's in a crowd or one-on-one.

I question whether love is a behavior you can learn. How do you express love to another person when you haven't experienced it? Thus, the question, can it be learned? In the deepest atoms of our DNA, we are hard-wired for love. Maybe love doesn't need to be learned. Love should be allowed to gently rise to the surface from wherever we keep our feelings hidden or buried.

We have commoditized the word love: "I *loved* that cheeseburger I just ate. You will *love* this new movie," etc. Love is defined as "an intense feeling of deep affection." As much as I enjoy cheeseburgers and movies, I don't have an intense feeling of deep affection for them and doubt I ever will.

The Greeks placed such importance on love they have four words to describe it:

Storge-which means empathetic love

Philia-friendly love. Where the city of Philadelphia gets its name (city of "brotherly love")

Eros-erotic love

Agape-unconditional love. Agape is used to describe love of God, children or a spouse

My first experience with Agape love occurred when my first son was born. In fact, the feeling was so powerful, it transformed me. When my wife told me she was pregnant, I was happy but not in the way I thought I should be. Many other couples were having babies the same time she was pregnant. The expectant fathers seemed to be so excited to have a child. I wasn't, so what the hell was wrong with me? I felt like I was supposed to feel some deep, intense love for my unborn child and I didn't. I was freaked out about it, and there was no one I could tell. I didn't want to be labeled a cold psycho, but I couldn't deny the way I was feeling. Every day she grew closer to delivery day, the more tension and anxiety I felt. My performance was worth of an Academy Award as I went through the motions of acting excited. What was really troubling me was this: how dare I bring a child into the world who may be doomed to feeling the indifference, abandonment and isolation I felt as a child? How could I do this? Looking back, my feelings were my way of experiencing love for my unborn child. I didn't want him or her to feel what I felt due to my own personal shortcomings. I was expressing compassion.

Delivery day came in a whirlwind. Adding to my fears, my child was going to be born five and a half weeks early! My wife was in labor, and on her second push little Charlie popped out, "sunny side up" as they called it. Immediately, upon seeing this beautiful, precious, innocent child I was overwhelmed with a feeling of love that came out of nowhere. I didn't expect it, and it was like nothing I had experienced before. This intense feeling of unconditional love consumed and took over everything in me. It was...transformational. I let go of the fear I had been holding in, realizing I could love another human being, my child, in the way he would need. He was so tiny (5.5 pounds). He had to go to into an incubator for a week in the neonatal unit. I followed him all the way there. I could not take my eyes off him. I loved him unconditionally.

Two years later my second son, Michael came on the scene. There was no nervousness or anxiety around his birth for me. I was 23 months into a relationship with Charlie, and I was crazy in love with this kid. I couldn't wait for Michael to arrive.

There have been times I haven't *liked* my children over the years, but I would never withdraw or withhold love from them. There are no conditions attached to my love for my children. As I have studied the character of God, I have found He is the same way. No matter how badly I screw up His love for me does not change. In fact, it *cannot change.* God is love and God is immutable. Immutable means incapable of change.

In 1 John 4:18 it says, "There is no fear in love. But perfect love drives out fear, because fear has to do with punishment. The one who fears is not made perfect in love." I am still trying to connect my head with my heart on this verse. It will come.

When I was raising my children, there were times when discipline was required. Discipline is rooted in love while punishment comes from anger and fear. Discipline is teaching while punishment teaches nothing. I am not suggesting my children liked being disciplined, but I would have failed them as a parent had I not disciplined out of love when necessary. My sons are young men with outstanding character, and I remain proud of them. There are still occasions I don't necessarily like them, but my love for them doesn't change. It can't. In that respect, I am immutable...

Forgiveness

On the morning of April 20, 1999 two dark and disturbed young men ended the lives of 12 students and one teacher before the two attackers took their own lives. At the time, the Columbine High School massacre was the largest school shooting in American history. In addition to the innocent murder victims, dozens more were wounded. Thousands of people's lives were forever altered that day from the slaughter of innocent people. One of those people is Darrell Scott, father of Rachel Joy Scott. Rachel was the shooters first victim that fateful day.

I met Darrell Scott on Monday, January 21, 2013 in League City, Texas where Darrell was scheduled to deliver the keynote address for The Amoco Federal Credit Union employees. Two things about Darrell struck me as we drank coffee together, getting to know each other. Darrell is one of the brightest men I have ever met. He is very well-read and communicates the knowledge and wisdom he knows well. The other characteristic about Darrell still amazes me. I use humor to get people to let their guard down, which I employed that morning. Darrell could genuinely laugh. He had a gleam in his eyes. I am not sure how I would be after losing a child, but the fact he could really laugh still stands out to me.

After Columbine, Darrell and his wife, Sandy (Rachel's stepmom) turned their pain into purpose when they co-founded Rachel's Challenge (www.rachelschallenge.org), the largest organization in the world focusing on kindness and compassion.

I never met Rachel and know her only through Darrell and Sandy. In many ways Rachel was a typical teenager with the ups and downs being a teenager brings. But Rachel was different with some unique characteristics you don't often find in teenagers or adults. She went out of her way to lead with kindness and compassion, mainly reaching out to three groups of students:

New students

Kids who were getting picked on

Special-needs students

Not long before her death, Rachel wrote a paper she called "My Ethics. My Codes of Life" where she challenged us to lead with compassion, calling it the "greatest form of love." In the paper Rachel goes on to write, "I believe if one person goes out of their way to show compassion, it starts a chain reaction of the same. You never know how far a little kindness can go." Since her death, through Rachel's Challenge she has been starting chain reactions of kindness and compassion all over the world. To-date, over 29 million people have experienced Rachel's story, and every year the organization receives over 150 documented letters, emails and Facebook messages from students who were planning to end their lives until they heard Rachel's story. Many times, the students were planning to kill themselves *the very day* Rachel's Challenge showed up in their school, until they heard the "story that changes everything."

One day in May 2015, Darrell and I were having a conversation in between luncheon and dinner meetings he was speaking at in Austin, Texas. Darrell is one of the most interesting men I know, and we can talk about a wide variety of subjects. At one point, we were talking about Rachel's Challenge' future, initiatives etc. and Darrell got reflective. He said something to me I have never forgotten, and I repeat it often. He said, "You know, John, all the good we've done, the lives Rachel's story has saved, none of it would have been possible *if I had not found it in my heart to forgive the two shooters who murdered my daughter."*

There isn't a word in the English language to describe a parent who has lost a child. I believe it is so painful there are no words that could fully describe the pain and agony.

Forgiveness is hard. We pathologically hold on to past hurts, giving them a life of their own. Not wanting to face painful memories, we bury them deep down, not cognizant of the harm they are doing to us. We must find it in ourselves to forgive those who harmed us, letting go of the hurt or we risk becoming bitter and angry. Bitterness and unresolved anger will shorten your life.

C. S. Lewis described letting go of the past like this, "You can't go back and change the beginning, but you can start where you are and change the ending." One day you are ready. You just know it. When you release the pain, you will feel like a giant weight has been lifted from your shoulders. You become free to live fully. This does not mean you forget what was done to you. You can't forget and shouldn't, lest it happen again. You view it through different eyes.

Forgiveness is for you, not the offender. The person who hurt you may not know they harmed you, and they may not even care. This is often the case when narcissists inflict harm. The narcissist only cares about self, creating carnage everywhere they go.

Self-forgiveness may be the most difficult of all. We know ourselves better than we are going to let the world know us. All of life's mistakes we've made are stored in our memory banks, and we stand ready to beat ourselves up about them on a moment's notice. It doesn't require any effort, either! We remember times in the past we made half-hearted promises to be better in the future, only to revert to past habits and toss another regret on the pile. When you find yourself beating yourself up, and we all do it to some degree, make a commitment to stop. It accomplishes nothing. Try being kind and compassionate with yourself. Forgive yourself for past mistakes, let them go and try hard to not make the same mistakes again. Being aware of a problem is the first step towards resolving it. Our words can heal, and they can hurt. Use kind words to others and to yourself.

The pathway to forgiveness is gratitude. Psychological study after study have demonstrated the biochemistry of the human brain changes when people practice gratitude, and it changes for the better. Our eyes open to the beauty of the world around us. We shift from looking inward to experiencing life more meaningfully. When we see the good in the world, we see the good in others. We can look at whatever it is we need to forgive and see the situation differently.

Through gratitude, I saw the shortcomings in my parents, their inabilities to parent well. I saw the flaws in their relationship skills and realized they didn't have the tools to be in a partnership with each other, let alone try to parent together. I saw their frustrations and how those frustrations manifested into irrational anger, and at a point crossed the line over to abuse, both physical and emotional. A part of their story was their upbringing. From what I can piece together, their families weren't warm and loving. They were isolated and cold. My parents followed their parents example, rather than working to be different. Their apathy eventually morphed into indifference where their children were concerned. When I saw their failings clearly, accepted them for who they were, I was able to forgive. It didn't happen overnight, but it happened. I cannot tell you how long your path of forgiveness will take, but I promise you this, you will reach the place where forgiveness happens and living life more fully begins. Nobody wants to face the inner darkness where the people who harmed us and their ugly transgressions reside. Neuroses originate from that world. The Swiss psychiatrist Carl Jung described it when he said, "Neuroses are a substitute for legitimate suffering."

To many people, practicing gratitude is a new concept. When I speak to incarcerated children about gratitude, they look at me like I'm from a different planet! Let's begin with something we take for granted. Fresh air! Take a breath. The air we breathe isn't toxic to our lungs. It's plentiful, and it's free! Children in Syria are dying to have the air we take for granted. When your "leader" has gas-bombed you, every breath you take sets your lungs on fire. As trivial as this example sounds, and because it is happening in a country halfway around the world, the importance of fresh air cannot be overlooked.

Let's add another thing to be grateful for, one a little closer to home. Fresh water! You can walk over to your sink right now, pour a glass of water, drink it, and the water doesn't poison you. It will poison you if you live in Flint, Michigan where the levels of lead in the water supply makes the water unsafe for drinking or bathing. The water in

Flint has led to multiple deaths. This isn't a crisis halfway across the planet, this is happening in the United States. How trivial does fresh water sound now?

As badly as I craved a normal family in my youth, today I look back with gratitude for the family I was placed in. I would have no credibility when I speak to kids who are in jail. They look at me like some older, extremely good-looking white man when I am introduced. What could they have in common with me? When I share my family life as a young person with them, they view me differently. I am one of them. One of my greatest joys is reaching and impacting these kids. I wouldn't be able to if I had been raised in a "normal" home. How's that for gratitude manifested?

I had to forgive God, too. I hated God when I was growing up. I cried out to him as a child to change my situation; help my family and help me. I was full of hate and rage toward the One who could make a difference. But He refused to. I couldn't understand why He wouldn't show up and help. I knew enough about God to know He could change things if He wanted to. One part of me was afraid to be angry with God. I knew He could do anything, including turning me to dust. I hated my life, but I didn't want to be turned to dust!

As I have learned about God's character, I know when I was hurting He was hurting alongside me. In His kindness He didn't vaporize me when I screamed at Him. The more I learn about the character of God and unconditional love, it frees me of guilt for hating Him. He can take a punch and not hold grudges.

Practicing gratitude might feel odd in the beginning. All new habits take time to grow accustomed to. I recommend starting your day thinking about the things you are grateful for. Write them down in a journal. Your list will grow as gratitude takes over your life. You won't regret it.

Forgive others. Be kind to others, and especially be kind to yourself. The world is a harsh place and can use more kindness. Change your outlook and change your life through gratitude. Change your future and become the person God sees you to be. It begins with gratitude...

Authenticity

How often do you hear someone say, "I just want people to be real with me?" We live in a world where self-reliance and its first cousin comparison reign. "Prosperity gospel" attracts millions of followers, promising you can have it all, while the purveyors of this "wisdom" sell millions of books. We know who is getting it all in that example. We embellish our lives on Facebook, showing the world our perfect families, perfect vacations etc. while others try to defy aging through picture filters and Botox. Does any of this sound like being real? No matter how hard we work covering up our insecurities, at the end of the equation emptiness is waiting. Still...

Do you think God wants us to be real with Him? We use our spiritual vocabulary using words like thankful, fellowship, pray, blessing and so on. Speaking this way doesn't make us sound more spiritual. If we don't talk this way in everyday language, it makes us sound like hypocritical idiots!

Remember the dinner scene from the hit movie, "Meet the Parents?" In the movie the prospective son-in-law, Greg (played by Ben Stiller) is asked by his amped-up, intimidating future father-in-law (Robert De Niro) to say grace before dinner. Eager to make a good impression, Greg puts it all out there! "Oh, dear God, thank you. You are such a good God to us, a kind and gentle...and accommodating God. And we thank you, oh sweet, sweet Lord of Hosts...for the...smorgasbord...you have so aptly lain at our table this day...and each day...by day. Day by day by day. Oh, dear Lord, three things we pray. To love Thee more dearly, to see Thee more clearly, to follow Thee more nearly...day by day...by day. Amen. Amen!" I crack up every time I write these words. He sounds like an idiot. I get it, though. Greg is out of his comfort zone. He wants to get his words correct put on a show.

I like to imagine God is laughing at this scene, too. After all, this scene is hilarious, laughter is good and everything good comes from God. But when we pray, do we sound like Greg? If I choose my words carefully, perfectly, maybe God will hear me this time and give me the answer I want. This is the day God shows up in a BIG way because I said everything right! We make deals with and try to manipulate our Creator. Then when we don't get the immediate answer we want our disappointment turns into frustration and anger. We feel ignored so why try? Is anyone even listening? We stop talking altogether to the One who can provide an answer, make a difference. We must adjust our expectations. Stop thinking God is some vending machine waiting for you to make your selection. He has three answers to prayer:

Yes

Not yet

I have a better plan

When we do pray, pray expectantly. Pray like you have already received what you are asking for, and believe you have it. Don't be timid. Be audacious! Visualize it, whatever it is, in your mind. Connect it to the emotional side of your brain.

When Jesus went to his hometown the Bible says He couldn't perform miracles there because of the people's lack of faith. He *could* do miracles but chose not to. Why display Divine power when no one believes? Are we guilty of the same in our prayer life? We feel good because we *remembered* to pray yet didn't believe anything would come of it. I believe God wants to show off His magnificent power through us. I base this off another of Jesus' teachings where He said, "If we have faith the size of a mustard seed, we can move mountains." I love this quote from Mark Batterson: "If our prayers aren't impossible to us, they are an insult to God." Remember, the power doesn't come from me and my awkward prayers. The power comes from the One who hears us. Be audacious!

Can you imagine marrying someone and never talking to them? You would be in a one-sided relationship. If we aren't speaking to God, we are in the same type relationship. In my own relationship, sometimes out of frustration I yell at God. That's right. I give Him my anger, insecurities, needs and wants full-on. I hold nothing back. Sometimes I question if God really knows what He is doing. If He does, then why am I not getting any answers? He can take it, and He won't turn you into dust because you got real with Him.

Rachel Scott, in a letter to her cousin, wrote, "Don't let your character change color with your environment. Find out *who you are* and let it stay its true color." Have you found yourself playing the role of chameleon, changing your personality to fit your environment? I believe most of us have done it. When you learn who you are, you no longer need to play a part like an actor in a play. You are free to be yourself, no matter the crowd you find yourself in.

We have dreams. Dreams about our families, dreams about our relationships, dreams about our future. Dreaming started as a child. Somewhere along the way we took an alternative road, a detour. What happened to childhood dreams? Real life gets in the way, but it's not too late. Don't let *anyone* steal your dreams! Reclaim them and feel your skin vibrate. You'll feel more alive because this is the *authentic you.*

We are unique. If you want proof of our uniqueness, look around. Do you see anyone like you? Of course not. There has never been another you, and there never will be. We are so unique by design even identical twins have different fingerprints. So why do we work so hard to conform, to fit in? We dress alike, we say the same sayings other people say, and we try our hardest to not stand out from the crowd. Rather we want to be part of the crowd. Then we have People magazine to thank for showing us who the really cool people are. If we want to be cool, too, we need to dress, act and speak like them. When we conform, we lose our identity, our uniqueness is compromised. We feel disillusioned and empty. We are disregarding what makes us special and giving our lives up for a hollow existence. Where is the authenticity?

The world tells us our value comes from our status and stuff, not from who we are. The message is reinforced every time we are introduced to others by our occupation or somehow labeled. "This is my financial advisor; this is my gay friend etc." Let me say it again: our identity is not what we do, and the world is wrong! So how can we change it? You can change yourself by altering your beliefs about what is important.

You cannot define yourself by what you have, and what you do is not who you are. Knowing who you are means you are comfortable with yourself, regardless of environment. I believe all of us share the same desire to be authentic and show ourselves to the world. What holds us back? Judgment? I won't be accepted? Don't like being out of our comfort zone? Maybe we believe if other people see the real me, they won't like me. There is an old song by The Moody Blues ("Never Comes the Day") with the perfect lyric: "If only you knew what's inside of me now, you wouldn't want to know me somehow."

One person can change the course of history. Thought and idea leaders like Thomas Edison, Albert Einstein, and John F. Kennedy knew who they were and knew where they were going. Nothing would stop them in their focused, single-minded pursuits. Today's leaders, Jeff Bezos and Elon Musk, these men will go down in history as individuals who changed the world. Maybe you have a dream you want to pursue. It gnaws at you; won't leave you alone; wakes you up in the middle of the night. Go for it! Give it everything you have, and don't let up until you have accomplished your dream. Don't listen to the naysayers or fall into the "what if" syndrome. What if I fail? What if people laugh at me? What if I go broke trying to do this? But...what if you *succeed?* What if you become a game changer; a high-level leader? First, you must believe it can happen. Believe in yourself. Bring your dreams to life, even when it seems no one else believes in you. You can do it.

The five men I mentioned pursued their dreams as their purpose. They refused to give up, even when the odds were overwhelmingly stacked against them. Every one of them had detractors and naysayers. When you are doing your life's true work, you won't give up either. It'll feel like you don't have a job. You will be working on purpose, tirelessly, and there will be no time clock to watch. You know you are doing what you are supposed to be doing in this life. When you find your calling, it takes on a higher purpose; a higher value. You just know it.

Part of my struggle with being authentic with our Creator comes from my earthly dad. He would punish me for being angry with him. Separating my dad's behavior from God's character is a lifelong pursuit. God uses discipline while my parents used punishment. The genesis of discipline is love while punishment is rooted in anger. They are not one in the same, although people occasionally use the words synonymously. I disciplined my children when they were growing up, reinforcing correct behavior. There were plenty of times my kids questioned whether I knew what I was doing. They had that right. If I didn't discipline them when necessary, it meant I did not love them. Parenting is hard, and loving another human being is hard. But love demands we do what is right, not what is easy. It is from this perspective we receive God's discipline; love. I do not claim to always understand it, or like it for that matter, but I am willing to accept it and believe things will work out for good. Somehow they always do.

Killing my father is killing the voices of doubt, worthlessness and failure he left me with. These voices guided some of my choices in my life, and some of those choices I'm not proud of. I cannot count the times I have been saved from my own stupidity. At least four times I should have been dead or disabled from brutal car wrecks. No one was injured or killed, which you would know is a miracle if you saw the aftermath of the accident scenes. Maybe I was spared to write this book. One of you who is reading this will take heart, face your demons, begin the hard work and heal.

Although I am still a mess, experiencing my share of failures and setbacks, more often than not wisdom has shown up in my life. I realize failure is not final, only temporary. The only failures in life are the ones who get knocked down and refuse to get back up. You always have one more round in you. Get up and get back in the ring.

There are two voices inside our heads, speaking to us, competing for our attention. Which voice are you listening to? If you are listening to the voice of doubt more often than the voice of confidence I encourage you to work on this. Willpower doesn't work. The harder you try to will something away, the stronger it gets. Focus on the things you do well. Keep your successes in the forefront of your mind. This will create a more confident mindset. We all have failures, but no one fails at everything.

Living with authenticity in a world which places more value on what zip code we live in rather than valuing people for who they are is challenging. You can do it, though. You might have to change some things, get rid of a few people in your life who aren't good for you, don't bring out the best in you. All of us march to unique drumbeats, and what a great rhythm it is...

Wounds

When the wounds from our pasts resurface, and they will, we have a choice. We can run from them, tamping them down with work, alcohol or other poisons. We wish them away, hoping they never return. For a while they will sink below the surface, but they do return, and when they reappear they are stronger and more forceful. Or we find the strength to face them, arriving at the proverbial edge of the cliff, contemplating jumping into the mess. Looking into the abyss of pain and uncertainty, we find ourselves ready to take the plunge, facing our inner darkness and work through the pain. Our destiny will not be limited by holding onto our painful pasts due to the failings of others. We take the scary, unsteady first step towards a better life, a healthier future.

In my case my wounds came from my parents. Both my parents told me "I would never amount to anything; I wasn't worth a damn." As a parent, I cannot imagine saying something so damaging to my precious children. My reaction to my parents was anger, which you would expect from a child. When I was angry with them, they *ordered me* to put a smile on my face or be whipped with a belt. Now I have been told I suck as a child, and my feelings weren't acknowledged. I still remember the rage I felt welling up inside me, not being able to do anything about it. When I was a teenager, combining rage with being a hormonal mess, it's amazing I did not go crazy. Add to the picture the humiliation and physical abuse I endured, I carried a heavy, unseen burden around as a child which stayed with me as I entered adulthood.

Anger and rage cannot coexist with peace and happiness. Something had to give. I gave into rage and hate. I hated my parents. I hated my existence, and I hated God for putting me in this family. Where was He? Was He enjoying watching me in pain day after hopeless day? I was full of defiance, too, not wanting to believe in any God who would put me in this family, but I was too afraid not to believe. One time I challenged God to come down and fight me (He didn't, and I'm glad). Being subjected to regular punishment for anything from accidentally spilling something to talking back was killing my spirit, but somehow I remained resolute I would get through this and get out. Life with them was unpredictable, without structure, and I never knew what to expect.

When I say punishment, I was forced to drop my pants, underwear and all, only to be whipped with a leather belt. My body would be left with welts and sometimes blood. When I was 12 one of my friends spent the night after a football game. We were horsing around, making noise like kids do when my father burst into my room, made me strip then proceeded to whip me in front of my friend. My friend tried looking away, but my father insisted he watch. The physical pain was awful, but the emotional hurt was unbearable. I was completely humiliated, and wasn't sure how I would recover. I was scared people at school would find out (the mind of a 12 year old), adding to my humiliation. Fortunately my friend is a person of great character. He never said a word to anyone.

I was hopeless, existing through life day to day, feeling isolated and alone. The façade I put on for the rest of the world that everything was okay I hoped was believable. I wanted everyone to think my life was fine, but in reality I couldn't wait to get away from this hell-hole. All kids need role models, someone to admire and look up to, but I had no one. Then I discovered Atticus Finch...

Atticus Finch is a fictional character from the book, "To Kill a Mockingbird," brought to life by Gregory Peck in the movie of the same name. Atticus was a single (widowed) father of two young children in rural Alabama during the 1930's. Based upon the author's father, Finch was a man of unshakable character who did the right thing, even when the right thing was unpopular and potentially life-threatening. Atticus showed up at the right time, and as odd as it sounds Atticus gave me hope there were good men in the world. He gave me the role model I needed, someone I could aspire to be like.

When I was finally free from living in my parents' home, I naively believed I could leave the pain behind. Physical wounds heal, but emotional trauma remains. I manifested my insecurities during my young adult life, and not in a good way. I tried everything I could to numb the pain, pain I wasn't acutely aware was there: women, money, status and stuff, but the emptiness remained. So I chased harder, looking for life abundant. The voices of the past remained, telling me I didn't matter, didn't count so why even try. Deep down I knew I mattered, but my uncertainty was real. Sometimes the fear I felt was overwhelming, almost paralyzing. I knew something was wrong. I had to do something about it or be relegated to a hollow and empty existence.

I began by reading self-help books, taking pieces from them which applied to me. Focusing on the positive pieces of myself and my life, I began to come out of the fog. It would last a while then I would sink back. This became a cycle I felt trapped in. I have a strong work ethic, so I persisted.

Fast forward to December 2010 when I was at my lowest point in my adult life. Due to circumstances I won't go into here, I had Post-Traumatic Stress Disorder (PTSD). Having PTSD, you feel like a walking zombie. Just functioning is hard. I wasn't ever suicidal, but every morning when I awoke I wished I hadn't. Every day I put on a brave face and faced my responsibilities, which included two kids in high school. I powered through. I was not living up to one of my life mantras: "Life is to be lived, not merely existed through." I was existing through, feeling nothing.

I wandered into Dr. David Clemons office on a cold December morning in 2010. David is a gifted psychotherapist, and it was no coincidence I found him. I knew I needed help, and my only trepidation was knowing it was time to face the darkness. I was a little afraid of what I might find there.

Early in psychotherapy, David suggested I had PTSD. Up until then I didn't believe PTSD was real, until I was diagnosed with it. David walked me through a therapy known as Eye Movement Desensitization Reprocessing (EMDR). Using EMDR, the therapist walks the client through the traumatic event which caused the frontal cortex to stop talking to the limbic system. You need both systems functioning properly for you to feel normal. PTSD is a coping mechanism for our brains, and nothing to feel shame about. After one session my brain 'rebooted.' It wasn't instantaneous, but over time I began to feel again. Only requiring one session was fortunate, but everyone's treatment protocol is different.

I am open about using a psychotherapist because I want to eliminate the shame sometimes associated with therapy. Engaging in psychotherapy doesn't mean you're crazy (some of my friends might tell you I am kinda crazy). Working on yourself is hard. Working on yourself is worthwhile. Remember the quote from Swiss psychiatrist Carl Jung once said, "Neuroses are substitutes for legitimate suffering." By suffering Jung means facing the inner self rather than letting it manifest into potentially destructive behaviors. The brain is fascinating, unlike any supercomputer ever invented. Our minds can work for us or against us. I prefer letting mine work for me.

As previously discussed, practicing gratitude was what allowed me to forgive my parents. Only when I saw them through the looking-glass of gratitude could I forgive their shortcomings. It will happen for you, too, if you try.

I encourage you to seek guidance from a trusted professional *when you're ready.* You are not being weak. Quite the opposite. It takes a brave person to face the inner darkness. Finding the right therapist for you is key. Keep looking until you find the person with whom you can build trust. Good therapists don't tell you what to do. Think of them like a tour guide leading you through a dark, overgrown jungle. He or she is the one with the machete, clearing the path while encouraging you to keep going. You do the work. They do the gentle nudging.

Keep going...

Purpose

According to the dictionary, purpose is defined as "the reason for which something exists." Have you ever asked yourself the question, "Why am I here?" If you haven't, you will ask because eventually we all do. We want our lives to matter, to have purpose and meaning. This is in our DNA no matter where you live. It isn't just an "American" thing. Mark Twain once observed, "The two most important days in your life are the day you are born and the day you find out why." A quick Amazon.com search under "purpose" in books yields over 50,000 results. The best-selling book by Rick Warren, "The Purpose Driven Life" has sold over 30 million copies and has been translated into multiple languages.

Who has the time to find life's calling when there are bills to pay, kids to raise, work to do, and maybe, just maybe we squeeze in a little time for ourselves? Living our purpose is imperative, though. Every year, Gallup conducts a poll about career satisfaction, and every year Gallup gets the same results: 70% of people are going to jobs every day they hate. In my financial advisory practice I started doing a non-scientific study of my own. Framing the question around retirement, I ask prospective clients what retirement might look like to them, how they will spend their time. Almost 90% of the time I get an answer that resembles something like this, "I don't know, but anything other than what I'm doing now." Most people I ask are facing another 25-30 years, maybe longer to keep doing what they hate. Quoting Maya Angelou, "You can never be great at anything unless you love it." There is no way to be effective if you don't love what you are doing. But people feel trapped by a lifestyle, and they are killing themselves to save enough for retirement so they can maintain said lifestyle. Combined with the fact people are living longer with the cost of living getting higher every year, it seems like a dead-end street. Where is the purpose in that?

People join cults because they want a sense of belonging. As perverted as it sounds, one of the attractions of being part of a cult is the people in the cult have a common purpose which unites them. This purpose binds them to something to live for, and sometimes something to die for. It becomes the most important focus of their lives. It's so strong cult member denounce their families or drink poison Kool-Aid to protect the integrity of the cult.

There has to be a better way. People are tired and people are stretched to the breaking point, giving themselves up to a life that leaves them numb...

Whether you believe in a Higher Power or not, all of us were created for purpose-filled lives. We are gifted in different ways. It is important to use your personality and abilities in areas you will thrive in. If you are an introvert, being someone who interacts with the public often may not be the best fit. Take an inventory of yourself. What are your strong suits? What do you like to do? If you could do anything on earth, regardless of pay, what would it be? These are great places to start.

Who are your role models? What is it about them that attracts you? Write their top character traits down. The reason for this is because what we see in others, exists in us. My adult role model is Ronald

Reagan. I have no desire to enter politics. What resonated with me about Reagan was his optimism, humor, his ability to communicate and leave you feeling better. These characteristics are in me. No ego talking, just facts. It is up to me to use those traits for good. If I allow them to go to my grave without fulfilling my potential, it will be a shame. So I speak. I speak to college campuses, incarcerated children, trade associations, even drug treatment centers. Spreading a message from the heart, sharing optimism and a brighter future and how to get there brings me more inner joy than anything. It is one of my callings.

Sometimes our callings are thrust upon us in an instant. Remember Darrell Scott from the chapter on forgiveness? Darrell was living a great life in the Denver area when his precious daughter was taken from him and his family. Darrell was able to forgive the shooters, then started an organization based upon his daughter's writings and life. Millions of lives have been impacted by Rachel's story. Two years after her death they found a drawing of Rachel's hands on the back of her dresser. Inside the drawing she wrote, "These hands belong to Rachel Joy Scott and will one day touch millions of people's hearts." When they found this, it had already come true.

Opportunities will come at you. It is up to you to take them or not if you feel them pulling at your heartstrings. If you choose to follow your calling, let me warn you. It will be the most difficult thing you have ever attempted. There will be roadblocks thrown in your path, and get ready for the spiritual darts: the dart of doubt, the dart of fear, the dart of confusion, dart of no confidence, and there will be times you want to quit. Don't quit. When you are pursuing your God-given purpose you will not fail. You can't fail. God does not create failures whether you believe in Him or not.

Pursue your calling with everything you have in you. Don't let your dreams die. I will end with one of my favorite quotes from Henry David Thoreau, "Most men lead lives of quiet desperation and die with their song still in them." Don't die with your music still in you. The world needs to hear from you...

Me

On April 28, 2013 I attended an event which altered my life. It was a warm Sunday evening, and to be honest I was not sure what the event was. Two good friends of mine invited me, so naturally I went. I believed I was attending a well-disguised Amway meeting. Seriously.

At the time I was divorced and had my eyes set on every pretty girl who crossed paths with me. I was driven by money, women and fun. I am not proud to disclose this, but I have to be authentic with you, the reader if I'm going to have credibility. Hopefully my willingness to be open and vulnerable will encourage you to keep reading. I had a simple approach to life. No complications. Just fun. I wasn't an egotistical jerk, although that's how I'm making myself sound. After realizing my marriage was not salvageable, I was ready to live again and thought my plans were what living looked like.

I met J Huffman that night, our host. It turns out the meeting wasn't for Amway. The meeting was to introduce us to his new business. I liked J immediately. He reminded me of myself: engaging, high-energy and...nice. We agreed to meet in about 10 days at a local Starbucks. Huffman's new biz was him meeting people where they worked, drank coffee etc. J would provide any spiritual counseling should you need or desire it. If you saw value in the time spent with J, you could go to his website if you wanted and make a contribution. No pressure. It truly was, and still is, a faith-based business.

I was the one who requested a meeting with J, but I wasn't sure what we would have to talk about. There must have been some value in what I saw since I requested the meeting. If we didn't find common ground, whatever that meant, I could give preacher boy a little money and maybe he would go away. Actually, giving a preacher money is the worst way to get rid of him. He will hound the hell out of you for more! Bad idea.

We met at the set time and spent around 45 minutes just getting to know each other. Huffman and me are both outgoing so we had no trouble finding stuff to talk about. Finally we were wrapping up. I looked at J and said, "You know J, I know God loves me. Any day I wake up I will tell you I am the most fortunate man on earth. But I am an emotionally driven man and I don't feel it. I know it but I don't feel it. Does that make sense?" J looked at me and said, "So you get it here (pointing to his head) but not here (pointing to his heart)." I said "YES!" J continued, "Well John, have you ever prayed about it?" "Well fuck no I haven't prayed about it. That never crossed my mind," I replied. I cussed purposely to see if the preacher boy flinched or told me I was headed straight to hell for bad language. He just smiled and said, "Well, you might start with that." No judgment for my language. No lecture. He passed the first test.

I did what he said, albeit my prayer life was (and still is) feeble at best. Every day I opened my laptop and Googled "God's love," and "Why don't I feel God's love?" I read everything I could, trying to connect my head with my heart but nothing was happening. Another frustrating prayer unanswered.

Late on a Sunday afternoon, I grabbed my computer and thought I would try one more time. I didn't expect a different outcome, just more of the same frustration. After five weeks of doing this daily search all I had to do was type 'G' into the search bar and Google took me where it knew I wanted to go! This day, something was...different. The second webpage listed on the first page of the search was still colored blue while the others were lavender. I thought this is odd. I went 6-7 pages in and every one of the web pages I had been to before. I went back to the first page of the search and clicked on the page (peacewithgod.net) and it took me to a well-done, short video. After watching the video, I went to the website it originated from. It turns out the website was part of the Billy Graham organization, and the video I saw was one in a series of short videos.

I queued up the first one to watch. It was set to soft music. Then you hear the booming, immediately recognizable voice of Billy Graham: "God loves you, and he loves you with a kind of love you don't understand. Because there is no human love like divine love." Incredible. I was almost in shock. My prayer was being answered right before my eyes. As I watched this short piece, there came a point where Graham said, "When Jesus Christ died on that cross, He did that for you. And He would have done it if you'd been the only person in the world." Out of nowhere a lightning bolt shot through my heart. I had never considered someone dying for me. I got cold chills and tears streamed down my cheeks. I looked up and said, "Thanks. I get it." The feeling has never left.

My life has been on a crazy trip since then. I still like women, money and fun. I haven't gotten weird. I am just me.

I hope my story has offered you hope you can free yourself from an ugly past. It wasn't your fault. You are here for a purpose greater than you can imagine. Don't let the failings of others hold you back from the life you are meant to live. A life of fullness, purpose and meaning. Please write me and share your story. I love hearing from readers of my short blog. I promise I will answer. Live fully, and live #purposedriven...

Email: rewrittenone@gmail.com

Blog: www.seeking-grace.com

Web: www.room340ideations.com

Made in the USA
Coppell, TX
26 November 2021